The current economy has presented many endless opportunities for new and existing businesses to position themselves to join in the next largest business revolution this world has ever known, and a new understanding of how business is done in the future. The unfortunate circumstance is that most people are trained as employees and lack the skill and knowledge of business ownership.

Although many possess the skill to offer a product or service, the mindset is geared towards, I will work so many hours today and get paid tomorrow. With this attitude they will find themselves in the unemployment line. So how do we deal with this problem? In this book we will walk through the steps of creating a business.

Hello, my name is Katrina and for me, God is the driving force behind every business that I have, I have been in business since 1998 and He has blessed me with excellent mentors, coaches, and business advisors. He continually aligns me with the right people, in the right place, and at the right time. My faith in Jesus Christ and the finished work that has already been done, entitles and grants me access to limitless possibilities in the business world. I am an entrepreneur, it's my birthright and God given talent to lead, train, and coach others into the destiny that has already been laid out for them. Three things I want you to see for your personal and business life. 1. The vision you have inside you. 2. Understand you can have it. 3. Knowing it will happen.

WHY BUSINESS OWNERSHIP

There are many reasons people decide to run their own business and no two stories are the same. For me, I was a single mom and needed more income than a job could offer and more time off to do things with and for my kids. At the time I was working what most consider to be an excellent job. I was the account/sales manager at a rent to own establishment.

My parents were well established and I never had a need in my life until I had children of my own. Here I found myself making, what most would say, "good money", but what is good money, if it's the only money coming into the house. I was working 40 to 50 hours a week but still I was able to draw welfare, which I did not want. When you are the only one your kids have, you humble yourself and sign up.

I drew a welfare check for four straight years and was able to come off of it, because I got a .25 cent raise, I was still able to get food stamps and the medical benefits for the kids, and after two more years I was able to come completely out of that system.

I always had a vision to own a business but at that time I didn't know what to do, so I tried a few such as catering, desk top publishing, babysitting, Avon, Blair products, Home Interior, Tom Watkins, Grit newspaper, Tupperware, CAN, jewelry, and clothing. In 1998 I decided to do something that I absolutely hated to do, start a cleaning business. What I found out, is I actually loved cleaning because I wanted to make things look pretty and I enjoyed watching the customer come in and be so excited and burden free. The story that really brought it all together for me was this. I had a client tell me that by hiring a cleaning service, it saved their marriage. Right then, I knew that I was on the right path. So with that all said and done, I started out wanting a better income. When in the final moment of truth, it was all about bringing change to people's lives. In 2005 I launched a coaching business as well. Both the cleaning and coaching business are still in full operation today.

THREE COMMON REASONS PEOPLE START A BUSINESS

I.   Financial Freedom
II.   Time
III.   Security

FOUR COMMON REASONS WHY BUSINESSES FAIL

I.   Wrong attitudes
II.   Lack of capital
III.   Lack of knowledge and skill
IV.   Lack of planning
V.   Procrastination

THREE VERY IMPORTANT QUESTIONS TO ASK YOURSELF

I.   Are you a self starter & disciplined?
II.   Do you have the capital?
III.   How will your product or service make a difference in the world?

When you answer these three questions, you will find your mission and vision statements. Answers like, "I want to make lots of money" will steal your focus and cause you to abort mission. If you're only in business to make a buck, you won't last because just as soon as you have a slow week or month, you will be ready to head for the hills.

You must also change your mindset from employee to business owner, because if you run your business as an employee, what you have done is given yourself a job. If you run it as a business owner you have now helped our economy by creating jobs. This is what you call entrepreneurship.

You will learn really fast that starting a business is more than just a great idea or more than you just being the best at what you do. Everything you have and everything that you are goes into building a successful business. You are on an emotional and financial roller coaster at times and wear every hat because there is no one else.

This is not to scare you away, nor to discourage you in anyway. I feel it necessary to tell people what they are walking into. In this book, I will try my best to break things down and give you as much as you're willing to learn. That is key, how much are you willing to learn, research, and give up just to make it work. Enough of me talking, let's get down to why you purchased this book.

The structure of this book may be different from other books you have grown accustom to, however, it's designed to be JUST SIMPLE!

Before you move forward, count the cost. You may have the money, customers, and skill, but if your home life issues are not covered, you will eventually spiral downward and crash. Let's go over a few, 1. Do you have small children at home? If so, what is your game plan for their care when you need to attend meetings and so on? 2. If you have a spouse, do they support your vision? 3. Do you have a full time job? 4. If not working, do you a have plan for paying all of your bills and still handle the financial side of your business?

You must be a self motivator and a self starter, because you are accountable for you now, there is no one above you. There will be times when you just don't want to get up, also times of giving up because you think you jumped in to soon. When starting the business, you will try to wait for the perfect time, place, customer and the right feeling. Don't freak out, all this is normal. Can you say, "Emotional roller coaster".

What we don't want, is for you to be complacent, or having continued thoughts of failure. When answering the questions below, be honest with yourself because this will help you be more aware of any weaknesses that would hinder your success.

WORK ON SELF! Which leads us to this next subject.

Do I really have what it takes?

Self Assessment Checkup

On most days, what do you wake up thinking about?

_____

_____

What are the content of your daily conversations?

_____

_____

How are you caring for your health?

_____

_____

What is your spiritual condition?

_____

_____

What books do you read?

_____

_____

Where do you hang out at?

_____

_____

How do you respond to correction?

_____

How do you respond to rejection?

_____

What is your life mission?

_____

_____

What are your goals?

_____

_____

Where do you see yourself in 6 months?

Where do you see yourself in 2 years?

Where do you see yourself in 5 years?

Where do you see yourself in 10 years?

Where do you see yourself in 20 years?

Change Your Mindset

What is the condition of your mind?

Definition of Mind: The human consciousness that originates in the brain and is manifested especially in thought, perception, emotion, will, memory, and imagination.

Definition of Set: To restore to a proper and normal state when dislocated or broken. (Definitions taken from online—The free dictionary by Farlex)

As we go through life, we pick up and experience negative events and thought patterns that we are unaware of until something jars our memory. The problem is, the mind cannot separate positive from negative. It just receives what we want to keep. Since most of us don't realize we are hearing and seeing negative stuff all the time, we don't tell our minds to reject it so it becomes stored on our hard drives.

LET'S LOOK IN THE MIRROR NOW AND WRITE THREE THINGS THAT COME TO MIND.

1.

2.

3.

What type of business would you like to open?

Is there a special skill that you have or a product that you want to create?

Do you have a niche that will bring a solution to a problem?

Do you want a traditional business or home based business?

A. Traditional business where you work away from home?

1. Rental fees if you don't already own property or have shared space available

2. Gas to and from

3. Utilities

4. Finding right location for your business type

B. Home based business

1. In your home (free space)

2. Don't have to drive in

3. Utilities included

4. Is your home easy to locate?

Service Business: You offer services.

Products: You have products to sell.

Decide now if you are going big or staying small. Now why do I say that? Because in the beginning, you want to prepare for the ending. So many businesses fail to put a growth plan in place and they miss out or accept an offer and not be able to fill an obligation.

Let me tell you what happened to me in my cleaning business. We grew from small to med size, and we were out branding and marketing the business, so much so, that before we knew it, we were a large business with only med size capabilities. We made it through the project because we did not want to inconvenience the client in any way. We struggled the entire length of the contract, because we put nothing in place for such a huge contract.

The client was well pleased with our performance, and I thought, "take a look behind the scene".... LOL... Now that could have gone badly, meaning, the client could have been under serviced which would have cost them time and money. This business is deadlines and timeline, so really there is little room for mess ups. So right now, look at your vision again and decide, "is this big or small?".

IS THERE A NEED FOR IT?

Do the research and see what type of market we are in, such as 1. Look at our economy and see what's in demand. (Remember you are creating a solution) 2. Is there a certain part of the world that your product or services are needed most? 3. Is it affordable?

What excites you about your business idea?

What were you doing or thinking when you came up with it?

What actions have you already taken?

How will you get others to get excited about your idea?

What will be the determining factor in them buying it?

Do you have competitors?

What sets you apart from them?

Your investment of money is not the only costly investment, but your time is something you can never get back, so make sure you do not waste it. This next subject will assist you with that. Have fun.

TIME AND LIFE MANGEMENT

We all have heard the saying, "There's not enough time in a day". We all want more time, right? More time to work, more time to spend with family and friends, or more time to enjoy the things we like to do. I'm here to tell you that there is enough time, but the problem is you don't know how to manage it. These simple 10 tips can assist you in getting on the right track.

    I.   How Do You Spend Your Time?

        A.

        B.

        C

II.   How Do You View Time?

        A.

        B.

        C.

What Time Does Your Day Start? _____
How Much Time Do You Need In A Day ? _____
Do You Have A Calendar? _____
Do You Use It? _____
Do You Miss Appointments Or Meetings? _____
Are You Late To Functions? _____
Do You Finish Projects In A Timely Manner? _____
Is Important Paper Work Often Left Undone Or Lost? _____

If you answer yes to any of these, that means your time is being stolen by something else and you need to get it under control.

10 TIPS TO TIME MANGEMENT

1. Prioritize – Which things have to be done, such as, appointments, meetings, events, jobs, and so on.

2. Use a calendar – Have a visual account of your daily and monthly task before you. (look at it before you go to bed and when you get up)

3. Create a daily plan – Some task you do know in advance and others you may not, but add your routine stuff on

there, (do this the night before you go to bed. If setting an appointment, you add it while making the appointment and or meetings.)

4. Delegate – Is there someone else that can assist you in any of these task?

5. Know deadlines – Always find out if there is a time limit or date on each task.

6. Eliminate Time Wasters – This could be tasks, people, or events

7. Be Early – Be at least 10 min. early, so you can find parking, the meeting room, and just so when you get there your mind is focused on what you are there for.

8. Learn To Say No – Everyone's problem is not yours to fix and every task is not for you to take on, and if you know you should be working on projects then don't let distractions take you away from your task.

9. Set Time Limits For Each Task – For the projects you have control over, you dictate the time frame for each task.

10. DOWN TIME – That speaks for itself, this is time where you are doing nothing, just clearing your mind and doing nothing. Sometimes this is the hardest task but I can promise you that it is the one that brings success.

THE DMS POD SYSTEM

Prioritize – To put in perfect order according to importance.

Organize – To put something into place in a neatly fashion.

Delegate – To release an important task into another persons care.

By putting POD to work for you, you will find your life being put into alignment like never before. Most companies do exactly that such as, Wal-Mart has the shoe department, sports, department and so on. Each one handling their own task without overstepping boundaries in another department.

When you first open your business, you may be a one person show, but after sometime, you will need a team of people that are part of your foundation, however these individuals need to be put into place beforehand. Follow the chart below and it will help you understand the power of twelve. This is not just for business, but also for your personal life.

THE TWELVE APOSTLES OF BUSINESS

Spiritual Advisor	Health	Business Coach
Business Owner	Business Attorney	Accountant
Tax Attorney	Banker	Financial Advisor
Insurance Agent	Marketing Coach	Personal Assistant

This is the team I call the twelve apostles of your business and the foundation of your blueprint.

If you have the mindset of, "I can do that myself", or "I don't need that", you will be keeping yourself in a job and never being free to build a successful business. This is the place where most business owners get stuck, and frustrated.

By using the DMS POD System you will find yourself FREE to move around the cabin of your business, remember, you are the face of your company and people need to see you.

List 5 Personal Priorities   List 5 Business Priorities

    1.

    1.

    2.

    3.

    4.

List 3 Areas You're Organized In   List 3 Areas You're Not

    1.

    2.

    3.

2 Reasons You Delegate   2 Reasons You Don't

    1.

    2.

How large do you want to grow your business?

Do you want employees?

<u>The rest of this is hands on</u>

A. Go over what you have in place right now and see if it is working for you.

B. See if it is you or your calendar that is not holding up to its part

C. Create a calendar

D. Create a daily plan

People tend that to think just because they have filled their day up with stuff to do and actually get it done, that they managed their time ..LOL..In reality what they have done was taken up time. The idea is to have more time, not use every moment of your day doing stuff, even though it all might be important. You need time to rest, no not sleep, but rest and enjoy life.

There is a huge world out there waiting on you to come and see it for the first time.   I really didn't learn this concept until I had to give up my time.

In 2008 I moved to Dallas. Before that, I managed my own schedule, or at least I thought I did. LOL... but what I had was a calendar full of stuff that was stopping me from living a life of peace. You see, when your calendar is full, you wake up ready to get everything on it done. Yes, you may get it done, but you did not have the chance to smell the roses. Back to the point, I had to go to work for someone else when I got here so my time turned into their time from 5:25 am to 4:30 pm I belonged to a system that told me when to eat, when to sleep, when to talk, what to say, when to laugh, when to cry, what I should feel, who I could friend, and how long I could do each of them. But hold on, it gets deeper, they told me where I could live, what I could drive, and the level of income I could make, yes I wanted not just time but my whole life, darn it, I wanted to live.

Since I have learned how to manage my time and life, I wanted to reach out to others who are going through the same old same old.

CUSTOMER SERVICES TRAINING

WHAT IS CUSTOMER SERVICE?

Customer--A patron, buyer, or shopper. A person one has to deal with.

Service--Work performed for another or a group. Assistance given to someone.   Goods or utilities that benefit the public.(These definitions comes from "The Random House Dictionary" concise edition.)

OUR DEFINITIONS:

Customer-- A human being, a person with feelings, your marketing department, your public relations department, your pay check, your raise, and your retirement.

Service--To treat people like you want to be treated, to give more to others than you do to yourself, and to expect nothing back for what you do.

REMEMBER HEARING AND LISTENING ARE NOT THE SAME

Your Customer Service department is a representation of your company.

Is customer service important? YES!!!

Is customer service everyone in your company's responsibility? YES!!!

BAD CUSTOMER SERVICE + CUSTOMERS = NO BUSINESS

AND IT YIELDS A PROFIT OF NO FOOD, NO PLACE TO LIVE, NO CAR, AND A VERY LONG UNEMPLOYMENT LINE (food for thought)

* Customers need to know that you have given them the whole truth and nothing but the truth. They like to be informed on every little detail. You should be well educated about your products or services and you should also share that with them.

* Customers like to know they have options or another way of fixing their problem

* They need to know that you are not talking down to them, judging, or criticizing them.

* Remember, you are acting as a mediator between the customers, products or services, and the customers expects to win.

UP CLOSE AND PERSONAL

1. Try to remember your customers name and faces.

2. Know what they like to purchase, what they like or dislike.

3. Develop a system that will keep you on your customers mind.

4. Let them know when specials, events, or new products or services are available.

5. Return their call promptly.

6. FOLLOW UP, FOLLOW UP, AND FOLLOW UP!

9 LAWS OF CUSTOMER SERVICE

1. Love: You must love and have a passion for what you do and most of all you must love you.

2. Joy: No matter how you feel when you get up you must put a smile on your face and be filled with joy.

3. Peace: Must have peace knowing that you are at the right place or in the right career.

4. Patience: You will run across some not so nice customers. Just remember that they are upset and you need to remain patient so you can discover the problem. They may not even know.

5. Kindness: When you get treated really bad, just be kind and remember, you can get more flies with honey.

6. Goodness: Always check your motive before you try to correct the problem. Ex.-- if you are just trying to fix it temporarily they will know. If you are trying to get rid of them they will know. You want to completely fix the problem so they can walk away trusting the company.

7. Faithfulness: Be faithful to self, business plan, and the customers.

8. Gentleness: When customers get loud , your response should be gentle.

9. Self Control: DO NOT FIGHT BACK!! This one speaks for itself.

Customer Friendly Atmosphere

The atmosphere we live and work in has a lot to do with our emotions, attitude, and our overall ability to think properly. At our businesses, we should be creating an atmosphere that will attract and keep customers. Here are a few things you can do.

1. Decorate in a soft way. (Make a statement that fits your mission)

2. Watch the type of music that your workers and customers hear.

3. The way you dress.

4.	The way you talk.

5.	The things you allow to go on there.

Some people may think you are going too far, but in many studies they have proved that the atmosphere of a business is very important.

<u>Lesson for the week:</u> Go into 3 different types of businesses and take notes, such as, the types of customers, how they talk, what's going on there, music, location, dress wear, and how they decorate.

<u>OUR THOUGHTS CREATE</u>

What are you thinking about when you get up getting ready for work?

If you are angry, yelling at the kids, lost items, rushing, and O, yes this one will get you, mad at your spouse. These things set you up for a bad day and a rude one at that.

What should we be thinking about? things that are true, noble, right, pure, lovely, and admirable. Anything other than these will cause you to lose it when standing there with an unhappy customer.

<u>EXERCISE</u>

How Are You Feeling Right Now?

How Is It Affecting Others Around You?

How Has It Affected Your Overall Performance?

STRATEGIC PLANNING

1. Develop a CS department.

2. Amount of money and time want to spend on CS training.

3. Set the standard for you company.

TECHNIQUES

When people see the technique, they should know it belongs to your company.

EXAMPLE: If you were blind folded and I took you into a Waffle House and you heard someone yelling orders, such as "hash brown smothered and covered" for a Waffle House regular, you would know that is their technique that sets them apart. Make sure your company has one.

ALWAYS MAKE SURE YOU ARE AWARE OF YOUR LEGAL RIGHTS AND THE LEGAL RIGHTS OF THE CUSTOMER. LAWS ARE CONSTANTLY CHANGING SO MAKE SURE YOU HAVE LEGAL REPRESENTATION FOR YOU COMPANY.

MARKETING
DMS WAY

Our goal is to introduce you to the world of marketing in ways this generation has never known.

What is marketing? It is the process of communicating the value of a product or service to customers, for selling that product or service.

From a societal point of view, marketing is the link between a society's material requirements and its economic patterns of response. Marketing satisfies these needs and wants through exchange processes and building long term relationships. - (taken from Wikipedia)

What is A Brand? It is the name, term, design, symbol, or any other feature that identifies one seller's product to make it distinct from those of other sellers. - (taken from Wikipedia)

To succeed in branding you must understand the needs and wants of your customers and prospects. You do this by integrating your brand strategies through your company at every point of public contact.

Your brand resides within the hearts and minds of customers, clients, and prospects. It is the sum total of their experiences and perceptions, some of which you can influence, and some that you cannot. –(taken from AMA)

Would you agree, that until you get yourself together, that nothing in your life will line up? In everything you do self must be disciplined.

Most people run their business like they run their life. That could be good or bad. Why do I say that? Well, ask yourself, "How do I run my life?" If it is good, than great, but if it is bad, can you say, "disaster". That's why in this book, I will always mention you changing you, well, the things that need to be changed.

When running a business, you must know how to communicate with people, such as your customers, employees, and business acquaintances. In order to do so, you must know you, like your weak points and your strong points. It is okay to admit you have weak points, because in doing so you learn to release that part to someone who can help you make your business a success.

LET YOUR PATH BE DIRECTED NOT DICTATED

I.   <u>SELF</u>

Character:

Language/ Body Language:

Appearance:

II.   <u>BUSINESS IMAGE</u>

Ok, now that we are going in the right direction, let's talk about the Image of your business, oh, you thought your business didn't have to look as good as you? Well guess what? Your business is a reflection of who you are. What you sow into it will be what you reap. What are you sowing?

Mission:

Vision:

Goals:

III.   <u>FAITH HAS FEET</u>

Do you believe what your doing will work? Then get to it. Building a business is like conceiving, carrying, birthing and raising a baby. When conceiving you had an active part in that. When carrying you take proper care of yourself for the baby's sake. Birthing it, you go through lots of pains and emotions, but finally you have to know how to raise it up to become something great. You can't just sit around thinking that he or she will just raise itself. You can, but what would be the outcome? think about that. If a child left to himself will bring shame on the parents, then what will a business left to itself bring on the owner? GET TO WORK!!!!

Research

Branding

Networking

I told you that this book would be different right? Well you know why? Because I am unique and so are you. True some things are just standard, but you still have to make your life and business uniquely yours, which takes us into a brief understanding of branding.

<u>Branding</u>

Three of the most popular and recognized brands in the world by people of all ages, races, nations, and generations. They are all addictive. Ask yourself, "why". 1. Each one of these, satisfy a void in our lives in some sort of way 2. Everyone else is doing it and they told you to as well 3. They are just excellent at branding.

A. Coke

B. McDonalds

C. Facebook

You see them everywhere you go. They encourage their members and customers to use them, as well. They just didn't stop there. They created slogans and other tools for people to always be thinking of them. So when you are setting up your business carefully, consider what you are putting out there because people can and will remember. Whatever it is make, sure it is not offensive, and too hard for people to get your point. JUST BE SIMPLE, but different. I like to say, "be uniquely you".

SIDE NOTE: SOMETHING YOU DO OR SAY MAY BRING OFFENSE DEPENDING ON YOUR PRODUCTS OR SERVICES, BUT DON'T GET DISCOURAGED BECAUSE YOU CAN'T PLEASE EVERYONE.

Creating A Platform

When no one wants to share their platform with you, what do you do? I tell you what you are going to do, you're going to create your own platform. Ok, you say what does that look like right? You must put yourself out there, I'm not talking about just anywhere. You have to understand where your target audience is and go where they are.

A. Develop a product that fits the message of your business and begin to put it in front of your audience, EX: I am not only a business coach but a life coach as well. I created quote cards with sayings and statements that I came up with. I offer them for purchase when I go to different meetings and events. This leaves an impression on the life coach side. What happens is people read those cards and realize that I do understand what they are going through and that I really do want to see them live a life of joy.

B. Host your own events. Once again make it about people and what you can do for them.

C. Get involved in your community, I would walk into local businesses and introduce myself and ask about city meetings and activities. Yes, you can find this out online but making face to face connections are priceless. There are other methods and so many to name. I would love to assist you with them. Leave a message on our website www.womenofabundantwealth.com.

WHEN NO ONE CARES BUT YOU

In business you will find that you may be the only one who is excited about your vision and no one cares if you make or not. Sorry to tell you this, but it usually comes from your own little circle. You heard me, but not to worry, because I'm sure at this point what they say or do has no direct affect on how you proceed, Right? Well I hope not. Be encouraged, stay focused, think outside the box, place no limits or labels on yourself, always, always dream and dream BIG. I pray this book helped you in some way.

I want you to write down what this book has taught you and live by it.